TOO GOOD TO BE TRUE

by Mary Hawley

Table of Contents

Get Started . . . . inside front cover

A Text Message Mess 2

Can They Make You a Star? 4

A Scary Scam 6

Respond and Go Beyond 8

    Stretch Your Brain 8

    Analyze a Pie Chart . . . . inside back cover

Millmark
EDUCATION

A Text Message Mess

Paula is visiting her grandmother. "Where's your new cell phone?" her grandmother asks.

Paula looks sad. "My parents took it away for a while," she says. "I made a mistake. I saw an Internet ad about getting text messages with baseball scores. The title of the ad said that the text messages were free. So I signed up for the **service**. But there's really a **fee** of $20 a month!"

"That's too bad, Paula," her grandmother says. "Now you know that Internet ads can trick you."

"I know," says Paula. "It was too good to be true!"

Talk with an adult *before* you sign up for a service!

Have you ever been tricked like Paula? Some companies sell extra cell phone services, such as special ringtones, text messages, or Internet games. Sometimes these companies try to trick people. They want people to think that these services are free, or very cheap. But when the **bill** comes, people find out the truth!

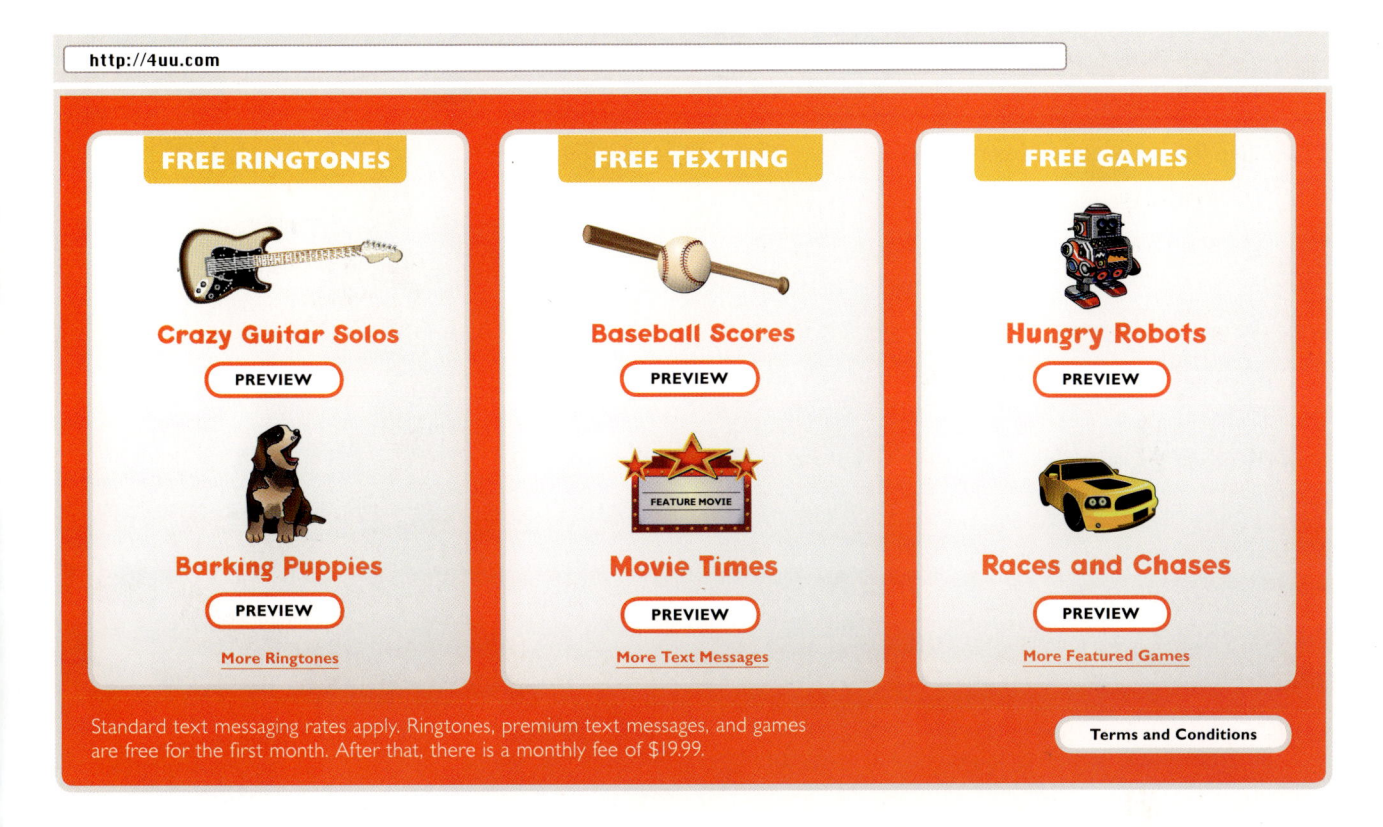

---

http://4uu.com

FREE RINGTONES

Crazy Guitar Solos
PREVIEW

Barking Puppies
PREVIEW

More Ringtones

FREE TEXTING

Baseball Scores
PREVIEW

Movie Times
PREVIEW

More Text Messages

FREE GAMES

Hungry Robots
PREVIEW

Races and Chases
PREVIEW

More Featured Games

Standard text messaging rates apply. Ringtones, premium text messages, and games are free for the first month. After that, there is a monthly fee of $19.99.

Terms and Conditions

Be Smart About Cell Phone Services

- Always talk to an adult before adding new cell phone services.
- Read the "Terms and Conditions." Make sure you understand the fees.
- Check your cell phone bill with an adult.

Connect Skills to Language

Paula's parents took away her cell phone for a while. Do you think they were right? State your **argument**. Then give **evidence** that supports your argument. Your evidence can include an example. Use sentences like these:

Paula's parents were (right/not right) because _____.

I think that parents should _____.

One reason they should do this is _____.

For example, _____.

3

Can They Make You a Star?

Sherise loves to act. One day, she hears a message on the radio.

"Do you want to be a star? Call the Big Time Talent Agency! We are holding **auditions** for popular television shows!"

Sherise is very excited. Her mom calls the agency and sets up an audition.

At the audition, Sherise acts out a scene. Then an agent talks to her. "Sherise, you have a lot of talent. We can make you a star! But first, you need to sign a **contract**. You need to pay our fees."

Is this offer too good to be true?

Sherise practices for her audition.

The fees are $3,000! Sherise and her mom are shocked. They do not sign the contract. Later, they do some Internet **research**. They find out that good talent agencies do not charge such high fees.

Talent agencies do help actors. But how do you know if you have found a good agency? The checklist has some tips for you.

Talent Agency Tips

- Good talent agencies usually do not charge a registration fee.
- Good talent agencies do not make you use their photographers.
- Acting classes are very helpful. But good talent agencies do not make you take their classes.
- Don't sign a contract without reading it very carefully with an adult.

Big Time Talent Agency
WE CAN MAKE YOU A STAR!

List of Fees

Registration Fee $400
Professional Photographs $600
Acting Classes $2,000

Make sure you understand the fees before you sign a contract.

AMAZING BUT TRUE

This tablet shows a contract that is more than 4,600 years old! A man sold a house and a field to another man. They carved their agreement on this tablet.

Connect Skills to Strategies

What is the writer's **argument** about talent agencies? What **evidence** does the writer give? Do you agree with the writer? To decide, **make connections** with what you already know. What have you heard about talent agencies? What do you know about contracts and fees? Share your ideas.

A Scary Scam

Emilio is a big fan of a Web site called Fuzzy Pets. The Web site lets kids create fun cartoon pets. When kids play games on this Web site, they earn Fuzzy Points. They can use Fuzzy Points to buy items for their pets. They can trade their pets and toys with other kids who use this Web site.

One day Emilio receives a strange e-mail. He reads the e-mail. "Wow, I would love more Fuzzy Points!" he says to himself. But he is worried about giving someone his user name and password.

To: Em333
From: A Fuzzy Friend
Subject: Free Fuzzy Points

Do you want lots of Fuzzy Points? Just send me your user name and your password. I will give you 1,000 Fuzzy Points every day for a month for free. I promise!

A Fuzzy Friend

Click here:
www.realfuzzypets.net

Emilio likes designing his own pets on the Fuzzy Pets Web site.

6

Then Emilio does some research on Internet safety. "This e-mail message is a **scam**!" Emilio thinks to himself. "Some group is trying to get my user name and password. Then they can steal my Fuzzy Points!" Emilio deletes the e-mail right away.

But this scam isn't just about Fuzzy Points. The link in the e-mail leads to a Web site. This Web site would put a secret program on Emilio's computer. The program could steal information about his parents' credit cards! Emilio is right to delete the e-mail.

Put It All Together
There are many ways you can be tricked about money. Do careful research before you sign up for a service. If something sounds too good to be true, it probably is!

Internet Safety Tips
- Never share your user names and passwords.
- Never give any personal information, such as your name, your address, or your school.
- Delete e-mails from people you don't know.

I DIDN'T KNOW THAT!
The United States government keeps track of Internet crime. In 2008, the amount of money stolen on the Internet was nearly $265 million!

Be smart about scams. Secret programs can steal personal information.

Connect Skills to Your Life
How does analyzing **arguments** and **evidence** help you:

- learn how people can be tricked about money?
- understand ideas in other books?
- make decisions after reading information?

7

Respond and Go Beyond

Share Ideas `After Reading`

What are some ways that people can trick others about spending money? Share what you have learned with a partner.

Connect Skills to *Too Good to Be True*

Analyze Arguments and Evidence with a Chart

Create a graphic organizer like this chart. On the chart, list the main argument for each topic. Then use the examples to give evidence for each argument.

Use the Strategy Make connections with what you already know about the topics and the examples. Then tell a partner whether you agree or disagree with the writer's argument for each topic.

Topic	Main Argument	Evidence
cell phone services (pages 2-3)	"Free" services may not really be free.	Paula has to pay $20 a month.
talent agencies (pages 4-5)		
Internet safety (pages 6-7)		

Write About It!

Write an article that explains why students should follow Internet safety tips.
- Present your argument about Internet safety.
- Give evidence that supports your argument. Your evidence can include an example.

Draw a Cartoon!

Stretch Your Brain

Draw a cartoon that shows a person being tricked about money. Tell a partner about what the person can do about it.